Learning to Read, Step by Step!

Ready to Read   Preschool–Kindergarten
• big type and easy words • rhyme and rhythm • picture clues
For children who know the alphabet and are eager to begin reading.

Reading with Help   Preschool–Grade 1
• basic vocabulary • short sentences • simple stories
For children who recognize familiar words and sound out new words with help.

Reading on Your Own   Grades 1–3
• engaging characters • easy-to-follow plots • popular topics
For children who are ready to read on their own.

Reading Paragraphs   Grades 2–3
• challenging vocabulary • short paragraphs • exciting stories
For newly independent readers who read simple sentences with confidence.

Ready for Chapters   Grades 2–4
• chapters • longer paragraphs • full-color art
For children who want to take the plunge into chapter books but still like colorful pictures.

STEP INTO READING® is designed to give every child a successful reading experience. The grade levels are only guides; children will progress through the steps at their own speed, developing confidence in their reading.

Remember, a lifetime love of reading starts with a single step!

To Maryann —E.S.P.

To Bob. Drop the donut! —M.S.

Acknowledgments: The author and editor gratefully acknowledge the help of Jayme Reichart, who has a master's in Egyptology from the American University in Cairo, Egypt. Thank you very much!

Text copyright © 2021 by Erica S. Perl
Cover art and interior illustrations copyright © 2021 by Michael Slack

Photograph credits: Front and back cover, p. 41: Stu Porter/Dreamstime; Front cover yarn ball: Sshleigel/Dreamstime; title page: Anna Krivitskaia/Dreamstime; p. 4: Ivana Tacikova/Alamy Stock Photo; p. 5 (left): Pavol Klimek/Dreamstime; p. 5 (right): Zelenenka/Dreamstime; p. 8 (left): Sanit Ratsameephot/Dreamstime; p. 8 (right): Ari Kustiawan/Dreamstime; p. 9: Lufimorgan/Dreamstime; p. 12 (top): Bridgeman Images; p. 12 (bottom): Tarker/Bridgeman Images; p. 13: Viard M./HorizonFeatures/Bridgeman Images; p. 16: Lucie Bartíková/Dreamstime; p. 17 (top): Shams Faraz Amir/Nils Jacobi/Dreamstime; p. 17 (bottom): Octavian Lazar/Dreamstime; p. 20: Wavebreakmedia Ltd/Dreamstime; p. 21 (top): Tatyana Kalmatsuy/Dreamstime; p. 21 (bottom): Thorsten Nilson/Dreamstime; p. 24: Juniors Bildarchiv GmbH/Alamy Stock Photo; p. 25 (top): Zanna Peshnina/Dreamstime; p. 25 (bottom): (null) (null)/Dreamstime; p. 28: Clara Bastian/Dreamstime; p. 29: Finney County Historical Society; p. 32 (top): Villiers Steyn/Dreamstime; p. 32 (bottom): Tjkphotography/Dreamstime; p. 33 (top): Shams Faraz Amir/Dreamstime; p. 33 (bottom left): Mark Levy/Alamy Stock Photo; p. 33 (bottom right): Elmarie Viljoen/Dreamstime; p. 36: Sourabh Bharti/Dreamstime; p. 37: Ondřej Prosický/Dreamstime; p. 40: Michael Shake/Dreamstime; p. 44: Okerele/Wikimedia Commons; p. 45: Eric Broder Van Dyke/Dreamstime

Visit us on the Web!
StepIntoReading.com
rhcbooks.com

Educators and librarians, for a variety of teaching tools, visit us at RHTeachersLibrarians.com

Library of Congress Cataloging-in-Publication Data
Names: Perl, Erica S., author. | Slack, Michael H., illustrator.
Title: Truth or lie: cats! / by Erica S. Perl; illustrations by Michael Slack.
Description: New York: Random House Children's Books, [2021] |
Series: Step into reading. Step 3
Identifiers: LCCN 2021004060 | ISBN 978-0-593-38032-1 (trade paperback) |
ISBN 978-0-593-38033-8 (library binding) | ISBN 978-0-593-38034-5 (ebook)
Subjects: LCSH: Cats—Juvenile literature.
Classification: LCC SF445.7 .P3725 2021 | DDC 636.8—dc23

Printed in the United States of America
10 9 8 7 6 5 4 3 2 1

TRUTH or LIE
CATS!

by Erica S. Perl

illustrations by Michael Slack

Random House 🏠 New York

Hi! I'm the TRUTH SLEUTH.
I'd like you to meet
some of my fun and frisky
feline friends.
"Feline" is another word for "cat."
That's TRUE!

But I spy a LIE nearby.

Let's play TRUTH OR LIE

and find it!

When you turn the page,

you'll see four statements . . .

BUT only three are TRUE.

Aw! Can you find a LIE
about kittens?
Go on and try!

1. Newborn kittens can't see.

Mama.

2. Newborn kittens can't hear.

ZZz SNORE

3. Newborn kittens can't run.

4. Newborn kittens can't communicate.

The lie is #4.

Newborn kittens can't communicate.

Newborn kittens
have lots of ways
to make their needs known.
When they are hungry or afraid,
they can nuzzle, mew, and meow.
They can purr, too.
This often means they feel happy.

Newborn kittens spend
most of their time sleeping.

They can't see, hear,
run, or walk yet.
They can't even
use the litter box without help.

Can you dig up a LIE about ancient Egyptians and cats?

1. Ancient Egyptians were the first to keep cats as pets.

2. Ancient Egyptians prayed to a cat goddess.

3. Ancient Egyptians made
   statues of cats.

4. Ancient Egyptians created cat
   mummies.

The lie is #1.

Ancient Egyptians were the first to keep cats as pets.

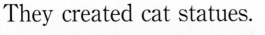
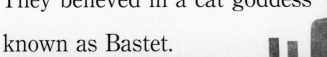

Ancient Egyptians were wild about cats. They created cat statues. They believed in a cat goddess known as Bastet.

And one of their cemeteries had
thousands of cat mummies.
But over five thousand years
before those
ancient Egyptian cats,
there were pet cats in Cyprus.
Other people in the Middle East
may have kept cats as pets
even earlier than that.

Can you pounce on another LIE?

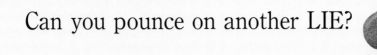

1. Cats can sprint as fast as

   thirty miles per hour.

2. Cats can jump up to

   six times their body length.

3. Cats have pouches, like kangaroos.

4. Cats almost always land on their feet when they fall.

The lie is #3.

Cats have pouches, like kangaroos.

Cats do not carry

their kittens in pouches.

Instead, they use their mouths

to pick up their kittens

by the fur

on the back of their necks.

Never mind, you've got it!

But they are great jumpers.
Cats have excellent balance,
powerful legs for pouncing,
and a reflex that helps them
land on their feet
most of the time.

Can you fetch a LIE about cats and dogs?

1. Dogs hear better than cats.

FOOD!

2. Cats sleep more than dogs.

TOP DOG

3. Cats have better night vision than dogs.

4. Cats need more protein in their diets than dogs.

The lie is #1.

Dogs hear better than cats.

A hertz measures

how high-pitched a sound is.

People can hear sounds

up to twenty thousand hertz.

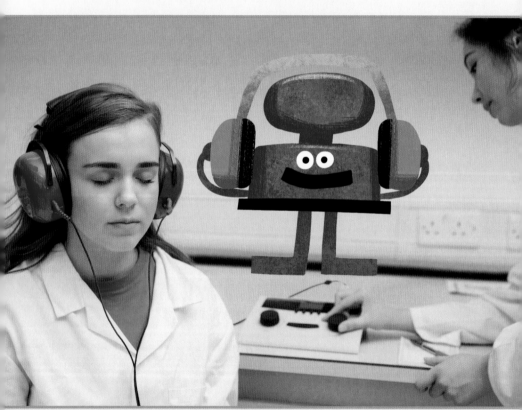

Dogs can hear
twice that well.

But cats win.
They can pick up sounds
up to eighty thousand hertz.
Meow *wow*!

Fancy a LIE about different cat breeds? Here you go.

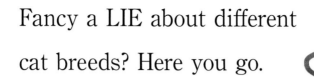

1. Many Siamese cats like to yowl and "sing."

2. Manx cats enjoy showing off their long, fluffy tails.

Ooh la la!

3. Turkish Van cats

love to swim.

4. Some sphynx cats wear

sweaters to stay warm.

The lie is #2.

Manx cats enjoy showing off their long, fluffy tails.

Most Manx cats have no tails.
Those that do
have tiny, stumpy ones.

Cats have many shapes,
sizes, and personalities.

Sphynx cats, for example,
are said to behave
more like dogs than cats.
They need warm clothing
because they have no fur!

Uh-oh. Did someone
cough up another LIE?

1. Cats have tiny hooks
   on their tongues,
   which grab hair
   when cats groom
   themselves.

2. When hair collects
   in a cat's stomach,
   it forms a hairball.

3. Cats are the only animals
   that develop hairballs.

I'm so jealous.

4. Cats spend almost
   half their waking hours
   grooming themselves.

The lie is #3.

Cats are the only animals that develop hairballs.

Many other animals, including cows, llamas, antelope, and chickens, get hairballs.

A museum in Kansas
has what might be
the world's largest hairball.

Impressive!

55 pounds! →

Imagine finding *that*
on your rug!
Don't worry, though.
It came from a cow, not a cat!

Can you track down
a LIE about lions?

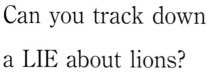

1. Both male and female lions
   can roar.

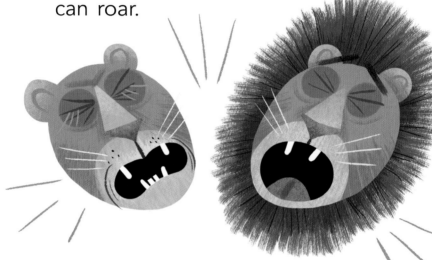

2. Both male and female lions
   can nurse their cubs.

3. Both male and female lions can grow manes.

4. Both male and female lions can hunt for food.

31

The lie is #2.

Both male and female lions can nurse their cubs.

Male lions guard
their pride's territory,
but lionesses
have important jobs, too.
They do most of the hunting.

They provide milk to the cubs,
which male lions cannot do.

Lionesses can roar loudly,
and a few
have even grown manes!

Wow!
That's a lioness?!

Can you spot a LIE about leopards?

1. Leopards have excellent night vision.

BOO!

2. Leopards often eat their meals in trees.

3. There are nine kinds
of leopards.

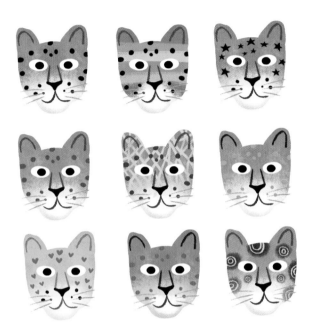

4. Leopards can only be found
in Africa.

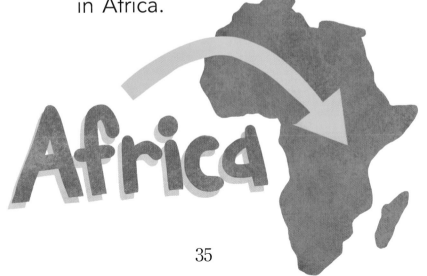

The lie is #4.

Leopards can only be found in Africa. LIE

In addition to African countries,
leopards live in
many places worldwide,
including Turkey, India,
Russia, China, and Sri Lanka.

Hanging out in India.

Many kinds of leopards,
as well as other big cats,
are endangered
and need to be protected.

Can you track down a LIE
about cheetahs?

No cheetahing!

1. Cheetahs can change colors,
   like chameleons.

2. Cheetahs cannot roar like lions.

ROAR!

meow

3. Cheetahs can purr like kitties.

4. Cheetahs can run faster than any other land animal.

The lie is #1.

Cheetahs can change colors, like chameleons.

Cheetahs have markings that help them blend into their surroundings.

But they are unable to change the
colors of their spotted fur.
Cheetahs might look
like a blur when they run
because they are so fast!

How about one more LIE,
about some one-of-a-kind cats?

1. All Ball the cat
   was the pet
   of Koko,
   a gorilla who learned
   sign language.

2. A cat named Stubbs was given
   the title of honorary mayor by
   the town of Talkeetna, Alaska.

3. The pawprints of Orangey,

   a movie star cat,

   are on the Hollywood

   Walk of Fame.

4. A cat named Ketzel won

   a prize for music she "composed"

   by walking on

   piano keys.

The lie is #3.

The pawprints of Orangey, a movie star cat, are on the Hollywood Walk of Fame.

LIE

Orangey,

who was also called Rhubarb,

did appear in movies

and was the only cat to receive

two PATSY Awards for his "acting."

But so far, no cat actors
have had their pawprints
added to the
Hollywood Walk of Fame.
Maybe your cat will be the first!

You did it!

You are officially a

TRUTH SLEUTH like me.

Keep up the good work!

- Read with an eye for TRUTH and a nose for LIES.

- Ask your parents, guardian, teacher, or librarian to help you find the best books and most reliable websites.

- Share what you know *and* how you figured out it was TRUE.

- Play TRUTH OR LIE with your friends and family.

Want to Learn More FACTS About Cats?

Books to read:

Cats by Seymour Simon (HarperCollins, 2004)

Cats vs. Dogs by Elizabeth Carney (National Geographic, 2011)

The Everything Book of Cats & Kittens by Andrea Mills (DK, 2018)

Wild Cats by Mary Batten, illustrated by Michael Langham Rowe (Random House, 2002)

Websites to check out:

aspca.org/pet-care/cat-care

cfa.org

panthera.org

petfinder.com/cats/